Hello, I'm a QUOKKA

MEET THE WILD THINGS

by Hayley & John Rocco

putnam

G. P. PUTNAM'S SONS

Hi! Hey! Hello! G'day, mate!

I'm a quokka. If you haven't heard that before,

it sounds like *KWAH-kuh* when you say it out loud.

Can you say it?

Humans who have met me say I'm the happiest animal in the world. Maybe it's because I am very friendly. My face just looks like it was built for smiling!

I am very curious, too.

What's your name?
Have we met before?
Do you like smiling?

I'm about the size of a house cat,
and I hop, hop, hop to get around!

Do you like hopping?
Hopping is my favorite.

quokka

I'm related to kangaroos and their smaller cousin, the wallaby, so I guess that makes sense.

kangaroo

wallaby

Female quokkas can give birth to a baby
about once a year. We call them joeys,
just like baby kangaroos and wallabies.

A joey spends about six months living in its mama's pouch after it's born.

See? Say hi, Joey!

Hi, Joey!

Most of the day, I sleep with a few of my mates
in the bushes, where it is cool and safe.

When do you sleep?

At nighttime we all come out
and forage for food.

I love eating leaves, grass, shrubs, seeds, and roots. Sometimes I eat snails or very small animals, too. But mostly I stick to plants and stuff!

If I can't find any, it's okay, because I can go for weeks without food. I store extra fat in my tail, which gives me the energy I need to get by. This comes in handy during the long, dry desert summers.

A lot of people don't know about me.
It's probably because most of us live
in a tiny little place called Rottnest Island.
It's off the coast of Western Australia.

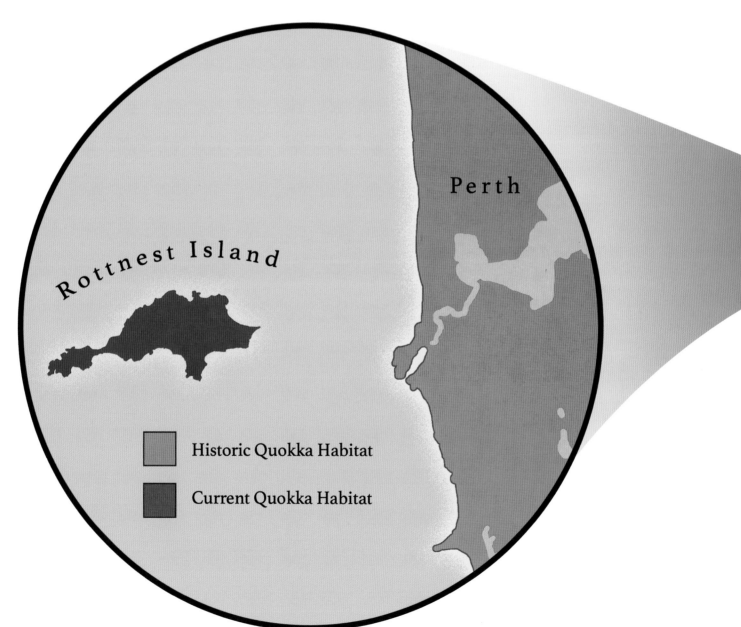

Rottnest Island

Perth

Historic Quokka Habitat

Current Quokka Habitat

AUSTRALIA

Have you heard of Australia?

We quokkas used to live all over
Western Australia before a lot
of humans from Europe
started moving here.

CAPTAIN JAMES STIRLING SETTLES
WESTERN AUSTRALIA, 1829

When they came, they brought foxes
with them to use for hunting.
That is one thing we do not like—foxes.

We had never seen them before, and
we simply couldn't defend ourselves.

Over time, the humans also started
cutting down trees and paving over our habitats
with their busy roads. Their houses and cities
left us with less and less space to live.

And if you haven't noticed, there have been
more extreme wildfires than usual, which means
we've lost even more of our habitat.

Now scientists are studying us to see how they can help protect quokkas like me.

Using special cameras and radio collars, they track
where we like to go and what we do when there are fires.

They are also working hard to eliminate
all the pesky animals that aren't native
to our land, like those hungry foxes!

Luckily, there are no foxes
or cars on Rottnest Island.
So we are pretty happy over here.

If you ever visit, be sure to say hi!

I'll be the one smiling.

A little more about quokkas:

- While most quokkas live on Rottnest Island, there's a small number still living on the Australian mainland and on Bald Island.

- The traditional owners of Rottnest Island are the Whadjuk Noongar people. They call the island Wadjemup, which means "place across the water where the spirits are."

- In 1696, Dutch explorer Willem de Vlamingh named the island Rottnest, which means "rat's nest" in Dutch, after he confused quokkas with giant rats.

- Rottnest Island is located eleven miles off the coast of Western Australia and receives around 500,000 visitors a year by ferry. Cars are not allowed on the island.

- While quokkas are friendly and approachable on Rottnest Island, it is important that humans do not touch or feed them, as they are vulnerable to human diseases.

- Like kangaroos and wallabies, quokkas are marsupials, a type of animal that carries their babies, or joeys, in a pocket of skin on their bellies called a pouch.

- Although quokkas have been called the happiest animal on earth, it is their natural facial structure that makes them appear to be smiling.

- Less than a month after mating, a mother quokka will give birth to a tiny hairless joey about the size of a grain of rice. As soon as it is born, the joey crawls into its mother's pouch, where it will live for the next six months.

- Quokkas can go for months without water by getting the hydration they need from the plants they eat.

- Quokkas are ruminants, which means they chew cud like sheep or cows. Chewing cud is when an animal regurgitates their food to chew it more thoroughly so they can fully digest it.

- Unlike kangaroos, which fight over territory, quokkas share their living spaces with other quokkas.

- Quokkas live for about 10 years in the wild and about 13 years in captivity.

- On the mainland, quokkas benefit their environment by consuming vegetation around swamps, allowing other creatures access to water and refuge from predators.

- Scientists have discovered that giving vitamin E to quokkas with muscle loss helps regrow their muscles. This breakthrough led to the development of a drug that has helped some young male humans suffering from Duchenne muscular dystrophy.

Why are quokkas endangered?

When European settlers moved into Western Australia, they introduced non-native predators like foxes for recreational hunting and cats for mousing. While quokkas have always had predators in the form of birds of prey, dingoes (Australian wild dogs), and snakes, these new predators became so numerous, they decimated the quokka population. Over time, the human population also grew and cleared out most of the quokkas' natural habitat, leaving them with less and less space to thrive. Additionally, climate change has resulted in longer dry spells, which threaten the plant life that quokkas need for food and shelter. The majority of quokkas now live on Rottnest Island, which has no predators but has limited resources.

In Western Australia, conservationists are working hard to control the non-native fox and feral cat populations to help protect and preserve local biodiversity, including the quokka.

Organizations working to help quokkas:

Australian Wildlife Conservancy: AustralianWildlife.org
World Wildlife Fund: WWF.org.au/what-we-do/species/quokka
Rottnest Foundation: RottnestFoundation.org.au

quokka

©David Wilding

For more information about quokkas and how you can help them, visit
MeetTheWildThings.com

For our brother Bill with the infectious smile.
—H.R. & J.R.

HAYLEY AND JOHN ROCCO are both ambassadors for Wild Tomorrow, a nonprofit focused on conservation and rewilding South Africa. They are the author and illustrator team behind the picture book *Wild Places: The Life of Naturalist David Attenborough*. John is also the #1 *New York Times* bestselling illustrator of many acclaimed books for children, some of which he also wrote, including *Blackout*, the recipient of a Caldecott Honor, and *How We Got to the Moon*, which received a Sibert Honor and was longlisted for the National Book Award. Learn more at MeetTheWildThings.com.

ACKNOWLEDGMENTS Our immense gratitude goes to the quokka conservation experts who are working in the field to protect these special animals and who so generously took the time to ensure we had the most accurate and current information about quokkas, including Dr. Shannon Dundas, Honorary Research Fellow, Murdoch University; and Matt Hayward, Professor of Conservation Science, University of Newcastle.

 G. P. PUTNAM'S SONS | An imprint of Penguin Random House LLC, New York
First published in the United States of America by G. P. Putnam's Sons, an imprint of Penguin Random House LLC, 2024

Text copyright © 2024 by Hayley Rocco | Illustrations copyright © 2024 by John Rocco

Library of Congress Cataloging-in-Publication Data | Names: Rocco, Hayley, author. | Rocco, John, illustrator. | Title: Hello, I'm a quokka / written by Hayley Rocco; illustrated by John Rocco. | Description: New York: G. P. Putnam's Sons, 2024. | Series: Meet the wild things | Summary: "An introduction to the unique characteristics of the quokka"—Provided by publisher. | Identifiers: LCCN 2023018801 (print) | LCCN 2023018802 (ebook) | ISBN 9780593618189 (hardcover) | ISBN 9780593618196 | ISBN 9780593618202 (kindle edition) | Subjects: LCSH: Quokka—Juvenile literature. | Classification: LCC QL737.M35 R65 2024 (print) | LCC QL737.M35 (ebook) | DDC 599.2/2—dc23/eng/20230501 | LC record available at https://lccn.loc.gov/2023018801 | LC ebook record available at https://lccn.loc.gov/2023018802

ISBN 9780593618189 | 10 9 8 7 6 5 4 3 2 1
Manufactured in China | TOPL

Design by Nicole Rheingans | Text set in Narevik | The art was created with pencil, watercolor, and digital color.
The publisher does not have any control over and does not assume any responsibility for author or third-party websites or their content.